They lived like this in
ANCIENT INDIA

Author: MARIE NEURATH

Artist: JOHN ELLIS

of the Isotype Institute

FRANKLIN WATTS, INC.,
New York

© 1967 Isotype Institute Limited
Published by Franklin Watts, Inc., 575 Lexington Avenue, New York 22, U.S.A.
Printed in Great Britain by Purnell & Sons, Ltd

Library of Congress Catalog No. 67-17660

ANCIENT INDIA

The area of present-day India and Pakistan is like a continent in
itself. It is surrounded by the ocean on most sides and cut off from
the rest of the world by mountains, amongst them the Himalayas. There
are as many people in these countries as in the whole of Europe, and
many languages, religions and customs. They have a long, varied history.

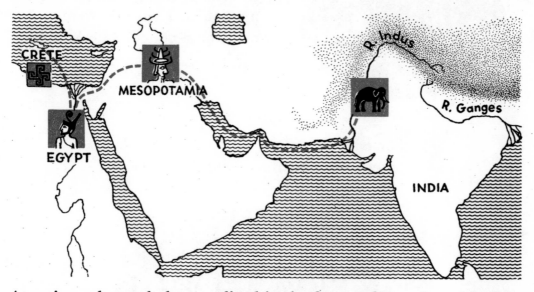

At a time when only hunters lived in the forests of Europe and India,
people in some parts of the world already grew crops, tended herds
and built towns, temples, dams and canals. The ancient Egyptians had
kingdoms on the Nile, Mesopotamians lived in temple cities near the
rivers Euphrates and Tigris, Minoans flourished on the island of Crete,
and near the river Indus, in the hot, dry country between the western
Himalayas and the Arabian Sea, there were great, well-planned cities.

This Indus Civilisation came to a sudden and unexplained end about 3000 years ago. From its ruins, which were discovered only in the last century, it can be seen that some of India's traditions began in this distant past.

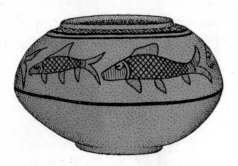

The remains of several groups of farming villages have been unearthed. Their pots were made on a potter's wheel.

Some are decorated with designs of fish, others show fishermen with their nets.

There were large pots for storage. Others had small holes in the bottom and were perhaps used for making cheese.

From the paintings on some of the pots it is clear that hump-backed cattle, which are common in India today, were already well-known to these early people.

Many small clay figures of animals, men and women have been found. The people seem to have worshipped a mother goddess and a father god. They also prayed to spirits that lived in the trees. Perhaps the bull, which is often represented, was a sacred animal. No remains of temples or other places of public worship have been found.

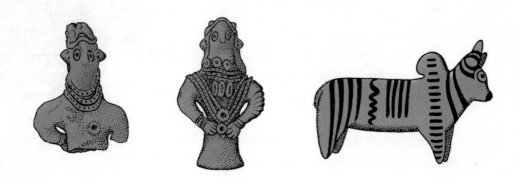

The large towns had a grid of streets, with living quarters for workers and houses for the rich. The houses were built of brick, and many of the better ones had their own baths. There were also large bathing pools, water storage and drainage. Altogether the towns were well equipped for healthy living in a hot climate. Grain was stored in large granaries.

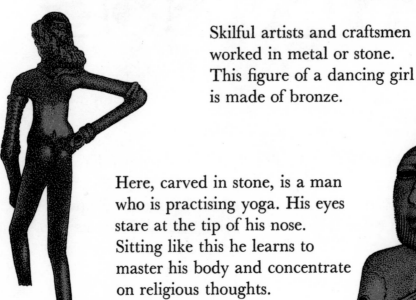

Skilful artists and craftsmen worked in metal or stone. This figure of a dancing girl is made of bronze.

Here, carved in stone, is a man who is practising yoga. His eyes stare at the tip of his nose. Sitting like this he learns to master his body and concentrate on religious thoughts.

Yoga has been taught throughout India's history and is still practised today.

The clover pattern on his garment may be copied from Mesopotamia. We know that the Indus cities sent traders there.

Mesopotamian influence can also be seen in the use of seals, and in their designs. Many depict animals like monkeys, tigers and crocodiles. The seals are square. On the first one shown above is an elephant, the animal for which India was famous even in ancient times. The second shows a humped bull and jungle fowl, the third a bull without a hump and some clear writing. We cannot understand Indus writing, because there are too few examples left for scholars to decipher it.

One seal shows a god with three faces, surrounded by animals. Thousands of years later the Indians made pictures of their god Siva, lord of the beasts, with three faces.

The Indus cities lasted for about 1000 years. There were no wars between them, and they never tried to extend their rule.

Then a great change took place in many countries, including India.
Tribesmen with horse-drawn chariots invaded the lands of the ancient
city folk. This new kind of warfare affected the whole way of life.
We see here how three different artists recorded their coming.

One lived
near the Euphrates,
another in Egypt, and
the third in Greece.

The newcomers introduced
the worship of the
Olympian gods in Greece.
They conquered Crete.

8

The invaders with their chariots and horses entered India from the north-west. They called themselves Aryans, and they were probably related to the tribes who entered Europe and introduced the languages that are still used today. These European languages have much in common with Sanskrit, the language of the old Aryan songs.

The Aryans were warriors, and their songs praised the gods who gave them victory. They had no writing and made no pictures, but their priests knew the sacred songs by heart, and taught them to the young.

They brought their families and animals with them, for they were wandering herdsmen who counted their wealth in cattle. They found themselves amongst farmers who lived a settled life, and soon they too learned to grow crops. They tried to dominate more of the land and prayed to their gods to help them:

> *We are surrounded on all sides by Dasyu tribes.*
> *They do not perform sacrifices,*
> *they do not believe in anything,*
> *their rites are different,*
> *they are not men!*
> *O destroyer of foes, kill them!*
> *Destroy the Dasa race!*

But the Aryans did not destroy what they found. They absorbed it. In many ways the conquered people whom they held in contempt were more advanced, so that while preaching their own superiority the Aryans were, in fact, the learners. Even their gods changed.

They searched the country for metal to make their weapons, tools and carts. As the carts could only go where the forests were not too dense, they travelled along the foot of the Himalayas.

They also went by boat down the great rivers, venturing into unknown land. Later they sailed along the coast, following the ocean currents and watching the birds to see where the land lay.

They learned to ride on the backs of horses and camels, and caravans crossed the hot deserts at night, steering by the stars.

They did find metal ores, and the greatest mining centre, just south of the lower Ganges, became the seat of government for the first great empire which united India.

Pieces of silver were used as money. They were stamped with imperial signs, which guaranteed the weight and quality of the silver.

Different emperors used different signs which scholars can recognise, and so we know the dates of these coins.

These men are
measuring a garden
with silver coins.
The owner has
agreed to sell it
for the number of
coins it takes
to cover it.

Over the years some of the dense forests were cleared and more villages were built. The houses were made of wood and clay and had thatched roofs.

Besides wheat and barley, rice was now grown. Here rice is being offered in a ceremony under a sacred tree.

The ploughs which they used were drawn by bullocks. They kept other animals like cattle, sheep, dogs, horses, ducks and pheasants.

Some of the villagers were craftsmen. Here two men are seen making a rope.

Ropes had many uses. This man is carrying his wares in baskets roped to a pole, which he balances on his shoulder.

This man is an arrowsmith. He is looking along the arrow to check that it is straight.

Each trade had a guild which arranged working hours and payments. Families followed the same trade, the sons learning from their fathers. Family life followed strict rules. Households were large, made up of many relatives and servants. The father, as the head, performed religious duties and was treated with respect. After the marriage of his eldest son he might leave home to take up the life of a hermit.

Everybody was born into a fixed position in society, so that the whole population was divided into rigid classes, called castes. People of different castes could not share a meal and could not marry.

The priests were the highest caste. They were not allowed to work, so the other castes had to provide food or money to support them.

Many lived as hermits in the forests, where young boys joined them as pupils, to learn the old sacred texts.

The boys also helped to collect food, and chopped wood for the sacred fire.

When, after some years, the young men were initiated, it was said that they "had a second birth", and they were allowed to wear the sacred thread. Some continued their studies in language, literature, mathematics, astronomy and medicine. The Indians knew surgery and the bone structure of our bodies and used herbs as medicines.

Not everyone was admitted to the schools. The sons of landowners, farmers and merchants could learn only some of the texts. The men in this picture are merchants, seen trading with foreigners.

14

Only boys born into the priestly caste or into the caste of soldiers
and rulers could study all the sacred texts.

The young man under the
parasol, accompanied by
a woman with a fly-whisk,
belongs to this second,
soldier caste.

The mass of the people, servants and labourers, were excluded from
all learning. Their hope was that after death they might be reborn
into a higher caste, if they fulfilled their present duties and led a good
life. They believed that they were born lowly because they had sinned
in their previous lives, and so accepted their condition.
Lowest of all were the out-castes, those whose work dealt with dead
men or animals. They crept through the back streets, or lived in
separate villages, because the higher castes must not even see them.

Over the centuries trade grew, in metal and ivory, gems and pearls, textiles and dyes, perfumes and spices. The first trade routes ran from the capital to the west coast, where Roman ships arrived, and to the north-west, where the Indian merchants met the Chinese silk traders. Later, goods were carried between all parts of India.

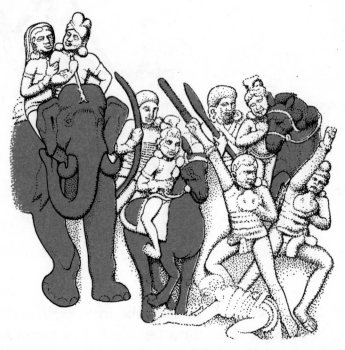

The emperors used their armies to care for the roads. Water was supplied, storage places and rest houses were built. The long caravans of ox-wagons were protected from hostile tribesmen by soldiers. The emperors even had forests cleared for new farms and roads.
Local groups were brought together under their government. They were harsh rulers and spied on the people to see that their laws were obeyed.

The new religions which appeared at this time also helped to break down barriers. They rejected the old local gods though they kept many old beliefs. They opposed the division of people into castes, teaching that all men had an equal chance to reach the blessed state through religion. They also objected to the slaughter of animals for religious sacrifices. One of these religions, Buddhism, became a world religion. Today it has many followers in countries outside India.

With the new ideas came new ways of teaching. Alphabets had been invented in Palestine centuries earlier, but the Indians would not use writing. Now this prejudice was overcome and they designed their own alphabets. One of the first looked like this:

Boys and girls were taught to read and write. These children, carrying wooden tablets and inkpots, are on their way to school.
Tablets like these are still used today.

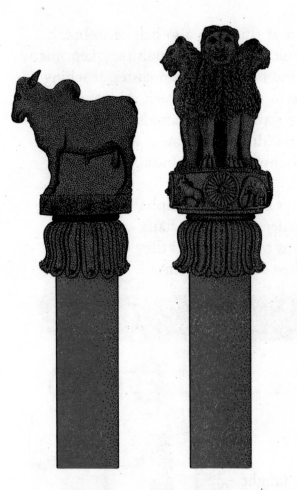

The first Indian books were written on palm-leaves or bark. Some emperors published their edicts by cutting them in stone for all to read.

The emperor Asoka wrote them on columns of polished sandstone like these, which he erected before city gates. On top of one stands a bull, on the other four lions.

Asoka, who carried on the wars of his predecessors, conquered and ruled more of India than had ever been united before. Then, suddenly, he realised with horror the suffering that his wars had brought to the people. He renounced war for ever. He would not even allow animals to be killed for his food.

Asoka studied the teachings of religion and put them into practice. He spent the rest of his reign looking after the welfare of the people under his rule.

His grandfather had earned fame by defeating the Greek armies which invaded India under Alexander the Great. Asoka now sent peaceful envoys to the Greek rulers.

At the time Asoka's capital on the lower part of the river Ganges was the biggest town in the world. The wall that enclosed it was 25 miles long. The town was regularly laid out with two main streets, which crossed in the centre, leading from gate to gate. The main gate was the one facing east. These gates were closed at night.

The town walls were built mostly of brick, but the upper storeys of the gatehouses were made of wood and clay. They contained the offices of guards and toll collectors. On the top floor were storage rooms for grain. The different castes lived in different parts of the town. Foreign visitors described the splendid palaces and houses along the wider streets. Nothing remains of them now, for they were built of wood, which was plentiful but did not last. The drawing on this page was copied from a stone picture made by an artist of the time.

Most of the pictures in this book come from the carvings on the walls of buildings like this, and from the richly decorated railings which surrounded them.

This is a stupa, a solid dome-shaped building into which a chamber was sunk from the top to hold a relic of the Buddha.

The dome rested on a "drum" and this was covered with stone pictures. They could be seen by people when they walked along the platform which encircled the whole building. Pictures of garlands carried by men and beasts are carved on the stupa, because garlands of real flowers were offered in worship.

No pictures of Buddha were made during the first centuries. In this picture only his footprints show where Buddha had walked over a lake.

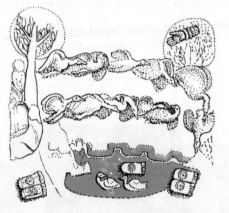

These symbols show the main events in Buddha's life: his birth (a lotus and a pillar topped by a lion), his enlightenment (the tree under which this took place), his first sermon (a wheel on a pillar) and his death (a stupa). It was believed that Buddha, having reached perfection, entered a state of eternal bliss at his death.

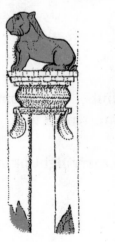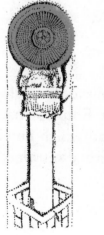

Buddhism teaches that souls are reborn until they reach the perfect state. They can migrate from animals to men, so an animal may be the present form of a future Buddha. In this picture elephants appear as worshippers, kneeling like men with their offerings of lotus flowers.

In the Indus civilisation an elephant was the symbol of wisdom.
In later times the Emperor had a Royal Elephant which took part in processions, and which he visited daily.
But elephants were also trained to work and to carry fighting men.

Men are not always shown as the masters. This man believed that the ram was bowing down to honour him—and it butted him.

In this picture, the antelope is a future Buddha. The other animals combine to rescue it from the hunter: the bird cries in the hunter's ear, to stop him, and the tortoise bites through the rope in which the antelope is trapped.

Among the scenes carved on the Buddhist buildings are many which show the worldly life that Buddha abandoned. From them we can learn something about Indian life of the times.

Here a rich young man is surrounded by girls and attendants amidst music and dancing.

Every dance had a meaning, conveyed by controlled movements not only of the legs and arms but also of the hands and fingers. The audience knew the meaning of each gesture.

The vina, which was played by kings and nobles, was the most elegant of the musical instruments. It had a wooden body with strings.

Two of these girls are playing harps. The others have flutes, which they are blowing in different ways, one through the mouth-hole at the end, the other by holding it crosswise.

A wall painting in a Buddhist cave shows a girl playing drums.

Caves served the Buddhist monks as homes during the rainy season. At other times they wandered through the country, teaching as they went.

Many of the Buddhist monasteries were built of brick around great courtyards, but the only ones which remain today are those cut into solid rock. Each monk had a small cell for himself, and there was a big assembly hall for prayers. It contained the shrine, a stupa.

The hall was dark, but light fell on the stupa through a horseshoe-shaped window in the entrance wall.

The cathedral-like hall was made by cutting away the rock. The columns at the side were shaped like wooden pillars.

Many of the caves were covered with paintings. Much of the paint has flaked off, but some of the pictures can still be seen. They show saints and people, plants and animals, dancers and musicians.

They also show the insides of rooms and tents. Pillars like these may have supported the ceilings in Asoka's palace.

In the monasteries the monks' life was strictly regulated: prayers had to be offered at special times, and the only meal was at noon. Instead of 24 hours they had 32. They measured time with the help of a waterclock, a cup floating in water. It had a hole in the bottom so that it filled and sank every "hour".

Under foreign influence the Indians began to make figures of the Buddha, and there were many pictures of him on later buildings.

He is often shown preaching, and the position of his hands shows what his sermon is about.

This statue is cast in bronze and is more than life-size.

From north-west India, where craftsmen were still under Greek influence, Buddhist teachings and art were carried to Central and Eastern Asia.

In India the empire fell and was replaced by many local powers with local religions. The beliefs of the ancient priests were now revived as Hinduism, enriched by Buddhist ideas.

The old village gods were represented in stone and metal, and new ones were added. This is a bronze figure of Siva, who is sometimes the god of destruction, sometimes the high lord of the beasts. Here he is shown as the divine dancer with four arms, holding a destroying flame in one hand and a bell in another. He is surrounded by flames, and crushes an evil demon beneath his feet.

The Hindus accepted that there were many forms of true religion. What mattered to them was that a man should bring himself to perfection. In this, Hindu and Buddhist aims were close to one another.

Some of the earliest Hindu temples were cut into the rock, like caves. In the main cell of one temple stands a large bust of Siva with three faces, recalling the three-faced god of the Indus civilisation. Thick pillars cut from the rock and decorated with carvings carry the roof.

Some tall Hindu temples were built of stone. Their great height was symbolic of the Himalayas, the holy mountains. They were covered all over with sculptured figures and ornaments.

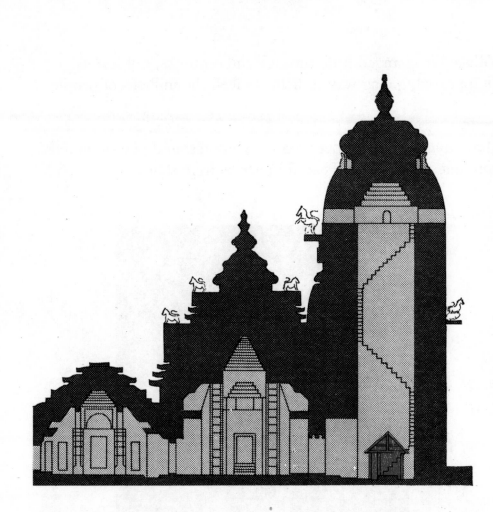

Under the tallest tower was a narrow dark cell devoted to one of the chief gods, sometimes surrounded by the rooms of other gods. Under the next, lower, tower was a porch which led to the cell. But the worshippers did not enter. They remained in the courts outside the temples, where there might be ponds for ritual bathing. The holiest water, however, was that of the river Ganges.

Village life changed little through the centuries, but forests disappeared, giving way to fields to feed the millions of people.

Many dynasties ruled over many kingdoms, and power shifted from one to the other. Peaceful periods were short.

"सत्यमेव जयते"

Nevertheless, the Indian leaders who preached non-violence and tolerance have influenced the course of world history, and it is fitting that modern India has taken as its emblem one of the pillars of Asoka, the man of peace.